"If Jerry Lewis had been struck by li̠ 35ish—*The Errand Boy* years, not the all the evil parts of his brain had been ̠ and his mother loved him more and beat him less, he might've written a book like *Sweatpants Paradise*. The speakers of Kyle Flak's poems deliver their soliloquies on the importance of hope and love and getting back on that horse after a tragic accident from atop an almost, but not quite, hardened surface of pink Jell-o, pulling out one foot as the other sinks, sliding once-twice-three times under the shiny jiggling surface. But they always get up, and slide back down, and get back up, and...'Are they gonna make it?' my albino python, Gina, asks, reading along over my shoulder. 'I don't know, but I hope so!' I tell her. Gina giggles, 'Kyle makes it look like even he doesn't know tee-hee!' 'Like a guy riding over the Falls in a barrel!' I agree, and we hug, and what a hug."

—Jennifer L Knox, author of *Days of Shame and Failure*

SWEAT

PARA

KYLE FLAK

PANTS

DISE

POEMS

Published by Gold Wake Press

Cover design by LK James (lkjames.com)
Interior design by Nick Courtright (nickcourtright.com)

10 9 8 7 6 5 4 3 2 1

ISBN: 978-1-64204-924-4

Sweatpants Paradise
2019, Kyle Flak

goldwake.com

CONTENTS

59 - HOW TO BE MY FAVORITE PERSON EVER

60 - IT IS DEFINITELY GOOD FUN TO PUT ON A WEIRD SMOCK AND PRETEND TO BE A WISE OLD SEA CAPTAIN BUT I BET THAT ACTUAL SEA CAPTAINS HAVE TO ENDURE SOME PRETTY TERRIBLE STUFF

63 - THERE ARE APPROXIMATELY ZERO ASTONISHING FACTS ABOUT RIBOFLAVIN OR OTHER B VITAMINS IN THIS POEM

MY VERSION OF AWESOME KARATE IS JUST EATING POPCORN ALONE IN A SEWER WITH MY DAD'S OLD CATCHER'S MITT FOR A BOWL

i think that this summer

will be really really really

something to write home about.

maybe i'll wear some purple sweatpants or win a can of baked beans

for guessing correctly

about just how miserable i am.

sometimes i look at my wife's new idea

about how to sell life insurance

to dead turtles and think

"okay i get it. we're not a real couple.

so let's just divide up our lawn full of dandelions civilly

like a herd of muskrats would."

actually, we've never met.

actually, she's just someone i saw on a mayonnaise commercial when i was trimming my toenails, so i said

"okay, we're married now."

then i fell asleep on my little bean bag chair from fourth grade

and don't remember what all happened after that, so

probably i am dying from many horrible things right now

like: enthusiasm for yo-yos, pajama deficiency, hot air balloon drama,

and goat envy.

i might wanna look all that up

on the speed stick deodorant website later on

to see if there's a kind of deodorant that can cure me.

but also, i'm allergic to all good things.

that is, i've never had quote "a good thing goin'" unquote.

i don't drive convertibles down to the beach

and lick ice cream cones mischievously

while suggestively petting my own moustache.

actually this is a love poem

for a very tiny stapler i once met.

one of those little tiny baby staplers.

the kind that always get lost in backpacks

or just thrown out

on the last day of school.

"who needs this?"

"oh! me! me! me!"

"okay, in the trash with you!"

and then it's all over:

this poem, other poems, romance,

maybe life itself

VARIOUS FAMOUS HALF-CONSUMED THROAT LOZENGES GLOWING WEIRDLY IN A SMELLY OLD COLLECTING JAR

i guess i just think that trees are so well-behaved.

they're practically spelling bee champions or model train enthusiasts.

the way they speak is like cutting into butter or vaguely sensing a ghost in a graveyard on the night you lose your virginity to a firefighter.

sunday afternoons are when she drifts into various bookstores and tea shops in a rare and magical dress that always breaks everyone's hearts.

"remember when lionel richie sang 'dancing on the ceiling' for the very first time in public and you were there smiling like an idiot because most of life is not as pleasant as that song is, remember that?" she says, suddenly vanishing forever because she's just a character i made up and i don't have the attention span to write actual novels.

these days i think about springtime constantly. springtime beside lake superior--what a dream. it is larger than most puddles. it is larger than most dreams.

i think that the weeping willow is my favorite tree because it most accurately captures the sadness of life while also being really really fucking beautiful.

oh, saturday nights at grandma's house watching the lawrence welk show and eating stale saltine crackers with butter on them!

oh, secret crushes from the mall, secret crushes from the grocery store, secret crushes from the abandoned doll factory!

oh, delicious canned ravioli products i have devoured alone while watching *Pretty in Pink* on VHS for the 84th time!

oh, everything good and interesting about visiting again that one special place where she finally kissed you, twenty years ago on a charming little side street now haunted mainly by old ass creepy owls and astonishingly sly silver maples!

i mean, there are just so many things in life that offer that rare short glimpse of the real deal, but astonishingly enough, we all still have no idea what the real deal really is!

i vote to say that the real deal should probably have something to do with trees.

i vote to say that the real deal should probably have something to do with clean air and beautiful nature.

i vote to say that the real deal should probably be a situation where even someone who has lost every arm wrestling match they've ever entered can still be respected and go up for an extra helping of dessert at the local bingo hall buffet luncheon.

i vote to say that the real deal should never involve throwing nice people into an alligator's mouth or letting a captain of industry decide what poor people are like.

but these are just some thoughts i had while eating a moldy slice of bread on a bench.

i am not an expert or anything.

i am mostly just alive.

I AM STILL VERY INTERESTED IN WHATEVER LOW-QUALITY MUSTARDS YOU MIGHT HAPPEN TO HAVE LYING AROUND THE PET SHOP BREAK ROOM TODAY

look at this stupid stapler

i bet it doesn't know anything about karate

"want to go eat some stale saltine crackers in a van
and then try to find a boring laundromat to hang out at for a while?"

that's my standard thing i say to a potential romantic interest
i don't even know what "romance" is

is romance a bloody banjo oozing purple mucus inside a slimy river full of
astonishing filth?

is romance an imaginary baseball game that no one is playing because
everyone has to hurry up and finish their taxes before the official april 30th
deadline?

sometimes i just sit in a corner and sigh all day long
sometimes i want to buy a package of suspicious eyebrows to put on my
bicycle somewhere

i mean what's this world coming to

this world has never even let me become the best jazz drummer in the world
and that makes me soooooooooooooooooooooo angry!

i keep trying to jump into the tv screen whenever i am watching the movie
Back to the Future on tv, but

i just get a sore head from hitting the glass on the screen

and i don't actually get to meet doctor emmett brown or mister marty mcfly

i just have to watch them

while they do incredibly exciting things, things i'll never get to do

aww, man / gee whiz!

i'm kind of going bonkers here

i mean one time in fourth grade my soccer coach said that all my dreams
could come true no matter what they were

but i don't see any dinosaurs in my backyard

i don't see any candy factories starting up inside my parents' basement

and my heart is one of those dead pickup trucks

that's just on a brown lawn somewhere for years and years and years

people drive by on sunday afternoons

and hope they'll never have a truck like that on their own damn lawn

but eventually they do

and some people actually think it's kind of cool

"you workin' on that thing? i got an engine in town

that could make it go like nobody's business"

ah, the soothing sounds of summer

stinky gasoline lawnmowers

angry beer drinkers

the frequent drip-drop of so many millions of sweaty armpits

lost lonely armpits

armpits of courage

armpits built to dream

LIKE MOST PEOPLE, I, TOO, WISH
THAT I HAD BEEN ACTIVELY INVOLVED
IN THE MOIST TOWELETTE INDUSTRY
MAYBE THIRTY OR FORTY YEARS AGO
LIKE MY DAD'S OLD FRIEND FROM TULSA
WHO NOW WEARS EXERCISE CLOTHES
TO SHOP FOR MICROWAVEABLE POPCORN

today i want to listen to some really great music
that makes me feel like a moldy surfboard
trying to ask a shy mannequin
out on a date
to the local sequin festival

okay, okay,
i choose New Universe by Desolation Wilderness
(KLP 205)
recorded at Dub Narcotic Studios in Olympia, Washington

i can't believe i am actually writing this
instead of putting my pants in the dryer

i will need dry pants if i am ever to venture out into the real world again
but i guess that's not important

home is where my CD player from the 1990's is
i wish i could say i've got a record player
but i don't

okay, wow, now "Boardwalk Theme" is on
i also like "Moon Dreams"
i also like "Strange Cool Girl"

this music is like the dream that i have about dreams where everyone is
dreaming

i think Ben Kopel would know what i mean
he listens to music

i've also heard that Anne Cecilia Holmes listens to music too
music is a good thing to listen to

so much better than the sound of nachos exploding in the microwave without
even getting eaten first--and who's going to clean up that mess???

i think it's fun to have fun
that is why i am writing you this letter

i wish i could get out of the habit of line breaks
and into the habit of writing bestselling romance novels that also become
good movies

where is that road?
it is not in my personality

my personality is Calvin Johnson's voice hosting a game show where everyone
just eats lots of bagels and then falls asleep

"you all win! everyone wins!"

it's so easy to type all this in autumn
next to a silent birch tree

i guess i'm pretty lucky
but the luck all comes from this great beach music

Desolation Wilderness, Desolation Wilderness:
i think i am your biggest fan

SWANS ARE NOT REALLY THAT ROMANTIC
AND ONE OF THEM ACTUALLY STOLE MY BROTHER'S
MINT CONDITION MILLI VANILLI CASSETTE TAPE
FOR SOME REASON

i'm a gross stinky box of gross smelly fish heads

i don't know anything about anything

everything i write is stupid

i wish i had more mayonnaise at home, but i don't

i wish i were that one girl in that one movie about sixteen candles called
sixteen candles

i think she's the happy type, once all her dreams come true

if i am already failing please raise your hand

then i can come over and disco dance all over your head

or mop the floor near your feet just to be nice

i think i should have been a dentist or someone who actually helps society in
some way

one time i made a slice of toast for somebody

perhaps that was my contribution

i wish i could help everyone in every way that helping can occur

i wish i could make a pot of gold out of a pot of slimy ramen noodles

i always keep coming back to thinking about food

maybe i could become a baker of really good corn muffins

which reminds me of this funny skit i saw on the conan o'brien show one time

it was called "the turtle who thought he was a corn muffin"

it was about a turtle who thought he was a corn muffin

which is exactly how i feel all the time

sort of

minus the turtle part

minus the corn muffin part

i only belong where i don't really belong

i only want to be what i can't really be

what a hilarious situation!

and the sun going down

on a dark sad

regular winter's day

so sad

i puke

SPOKEN LIKE A TRUE GLOVE COMPARTMENT

some dreams live inside a haircut

some dreams live inside a spooky ghost car

i wonder if i am even alive

i was happy in autumn one time

walking down the street

and she nervously grabbed my hand

like it was a mysterious cupcake from mars

hey what's the deal with sad lonely diners in sad lonely towns

what's the deal with the first day of school when you're not in school anymore

jerry seinfeld doesn't know

my hip cool dad doesn't know either

sometimes i feel like i am driving an annoying ice cream truck into an ocean made entirely out of dead leaves and professional cribbage players

my mind is never made up

my face is a pair of sweatpants worn to watch saturday morning cartoons and eat rainbow-colored cereals please don't beat me up with that invisible echo chamber again, grandma

someday i might fall in love

and make no one on earth

so insanely happy

BILL'S TWILL PANTS

Bill was unsure about his new twill pants. They had seemed alright in the store and everything when he tried them on, but now? Now could he completely say that he was completely satisfied?????

"Hey Bill, nice twill pants ya got there!" It was Cynthia. Was she being serious or was she only mocking him. The pants were a robust orange color, loose, and covered in decorative 3-D coins.

"Really? You really mean it, Cynthia? I just thought they were kind of neat so I bought them."

They were both walking past a pizza place on the boardwalk on the Jersey shore. It was astonishing to think that there might be sharks nearby! All anyone could see were surfers in the mist, though.

"Yeah. I really like them. They remind me of a happier era--like summer vacation when we were both just kids." Cynthia was a forty-something-year-old insurance saleswoman. She seemed to have settled in just fine to the middle years of life, but???????

"Oh, thanks. Thanks. I'm glad you like them."

Bill was happy to bump into her, but also nervous. He was wondering if he could maybe talk her into enjoying a nice slice of anchovy pizza with him at his favorite place. Maybe the pants had magical powers or something. Maybe the pants could help him make all his dreams come true!

"Yeah. They're really neat pants, Bill. Wanna go grab a slice of anchovy pizza over at your favorite little place that's right over there practically right in front of us right now?" Cynthia asked.

What??????

The pants were magical, then!!!!!

Bill patted himself on his own rump like he had done a good job in football or something. He was happy, but it was kind of scary just walking around in a pair of magical pants.

"I had better be careful," he thought to himself.

"No! Be reckless and fun just like me!" said the magical pair of pants in a voice that only Bill could hear.

Oh no. It was starting. Life was changing all over again in an instant.

GO ON, PET MY SAD KIWI'S FINE BROWN HAIR LIKE IT'S GOT SOMETHING NEW TO TEACH YOU ABOUT HOW TO WIN FIVE NEW BOWLING TROPHIES WITHOUT REALLY TRYING

it is summer and i'm as lonely as a buccaneer stuck inside a painting.

the boring baseball card sky is full of pretty sunshine,

everyone's ugly lawn is full of cute baby bunny rabbits dressed in

charming little detective trench coats,

and just five minutes ago, i mastered every yo-yo trick in the book,

but who's really watching?

and also: who's honestly interested in yo-yos?

i guess what i'm trying to say is: it's probably a really good time to make a huge taco salad or something.

i guess what i'm trying to say is: it's probably the best possible time to build a happy army of fake friends out of this moldy pile of autumn leaves i found out back behind augusta, maine's spookiest cemetery.

the world is whatever kurt cobain said it was back in 1992 when i was a grunge rocker too.

we were all little grunge rockers then. the idea was: music lives inside a lumberjack's sad chainsaw when it's raining inside a coffeehouse at 3 a.m. in the pacific northwest and also your dad's a mean volunteer archery coach with arteriosclerosis.

additionally, i just noticed: the fees on my bank statement. i don't know what they are for.

i wish i were a tiny toy unicorn running around in somebody else's dream about tiny toy unicorns.

i don't know why i just said that. i am really more of a burlap sack left out in the desert with nothing in it.

maybe my old memories will sustain me like oompa loompas sustain willy wonka's chocolate factory.

for instance, i used to be pretty good at making out with couch cushions. that's pretty good, right?

somebody please wake me up.

somebody please tell me i am sorry for never really living and stuff.

i want to walk to the store and walk to the park using my mind so that i don't have to actually leave this super cozy blanket and chair fort i built for myself out here in the family room.

okay, now i am doing it.

okay, now i'm back.

but: where are all the pencils i pretended to purchase?

and where are all the welsh corgis who remembered to bark at me because i am so suspicious and scary?

well, good, then.

nothing really happened so i am still myself then.

i hope that i can continue doing this forever.

by "this," i mean this documenting of things that have no value to anyone.

i feel like someone who's falling in love during a certain special part of a certain special movie.

i could sing and dance in the street.

but instead i will probably just curl up into a tiny little ball

and dream that i am roasting marshmallows in the forest with keanu reeves, my psychiatrist, and legendary miami dolphins football legend dan marino.

but what if i die before i ever get to write any new and improved poems?

well, then, just watch a bunch of damn keanu reeves movies without me then.

i am pretty sure that the rest of my poems were just going to be rewrites of *bill and ted's excellent adventure* anyway.

RETURN TO THE ESCAPE FROM THE HAUNTED CITY OF FRIGHT AND DOOM COMES BACK!

I really love eating massive bowls of cereal while climbing up the Eiffel Tower with a grappling hook. Today is Tuesday April 47th, nineteen hundred and four thousand, but I don't really care what day it is. I just want Vikings, robots, saber-toothed tigers, disco dancing, Mickey Mantle, corn on the cob, and everything else to all be in this together. I just want to imagine new kinds of bowling ball bags to put all my favorite memories from my senior prom in. This record player is a bowling ball bag. This delicious slice of homemade rhubarb pie is a bowling ball bag. Some bowling ball bags want to take away all your money and also end your life. Those bowling ball bags are called "that one guy I met one time in Reno, Nevada at three a.m. on the roof of this really great pancake house just after I had woken up from a pretty okay nap I took inside some fluffy melting tar I found over on the east side of the roof right beside the chimney." Sometimes people think that I am just another smelly rucksack full of crying circus peanuts. They think that life is all about how you hold your catcher's mitt and where the map to the secret pirate treasure chest said you should go. But my catcher's mitt is made out of fire trucks that are also full of ghosts that also laugh and sing Mariah Carey songs all night long, so I still don't know why anybody would care about what the heck I do for thrills. Spooky night beside some swaying cornstalks. Lazy day inside a pawn shop canary cage playing with yo-yos. Dream any dream. Do somersaults naked in a tan van going five miles per hour in a virtual reality machine outside a shoe store. This is your one and only life and I am tired of telling you guys that. It's like every poem is just a poor substitute for Robin Williams' wonderful performance in the smash hit summer goofball comedy *Dead Poet's Society*. And yet I go on, writing more poems, making more smash hit summer goofball comedies in my backyard with this broken camera from the clearance bin. Hope you don't mind/notice. I was only planning to scribble for a couple of seconds on some stupid napkins in the back of some stupid diner,

24

but then slowly, little by little I guess I ran out of napkins, so now I am here. Look out world.

THE TROUBLING CASE OF JOHN CUSACK AND THE GHOST PIE

i find a pie on a windowsill
but this is up in ghost country
so it might just be a ghost
that's pretending to be a pie

i wait in a lake with john cusack
to try and figure out this
weird exciting mystery

"you goin' bowling on saturday?" says john cusack
"nope," i say
"awww man!" says john cusack

night at the lake!

i brush my hair using an old candlestick wall telephone
i found in the lake

what was that thing i came here to do?

gradually with no effort at all,
i put on some lawrence welk music
to try and relax

it's fun in a lake

have you heard about s'mores?

they are a popular treat for hungry campers

but i feel like john cusack isn't even here anymore

sometimes he has to leave
to come back taller
and more vaguely in love
with his own sensitivity

moon above a pontoon
eerie screams that sound like pies

i don't know what this place is

i don't know why the movie actually chose to put me here

YOU COLLECT BLAND PLACE MATS
FROM VARIOUS BORING LOCATIONS

Your favorite word is "the." No one enjoys escalator rides more than you do when an escalator is broken and you have to walk up it: "Yay! Finally, it's just regular stairs again. Now no one will get to have any sexy good times or go anywhere faster," you say out loud and then laugh demonically. To you, kangaroos seem irrelevant, indulgent, and obnoxiously energetic. You wish that everything would just wear a proper necktie and sunscreen. These days, your lawn and driveway mean more to you than anybody's first major kiss in high school. You have thought of getting your lawn a Christmas present. You have thought of going over your driveway with a toothbrush just to make sure it's absolutely sanitary. Whenever disco music is played anywhere, you hide under a chair and cry until it's over. You allow yourself just one plain doughnut per month and you eat it soundlessly while reading a dreadfully crisp newspaper in a respectable and affordable little cafeteria where your grandma used to go to play bingo. "Is everything terrible?" is a question that you don't allow yourself to think about, but you do often feel it in your blood, especially when you are forced to ride in an airplane for several hours with a herd of strangers who might have various enthusiasms and passions that go way beyond anything you ever felt when you were at the miniature golf course for five minutes on a Saturday in July one time and actually briefly had an okay time you guess.

TRY TRADING A BEAVER PELT
FOR A SUPER BIG GULP MOUNTAIN DEW SLURPIE
AT 7-ELEVEN,
YEAH, JUST TRY IT

her sweater is the record shop i always dreamed about
in my pathetic loser brain

i walk downtown
remembering every autumn i've ever loved

blue heron by the river!
rubber cement in office supply store window!
fuzzy puppet walking to work at the fuzzy puppet employment center!

hey, let's do that one insane sandwich thing we do
where we order one of every sandwich they have somewhere

it seems like just yesterday
we were always surfing in a wild pool of wild teenage love
mint condition
years ago
blue blue love
delicious candy from a super deluxe hidden spaceship made out of drunk
electric guitarists from a secret planet

i want to put our first kiss in my wallet
and never really spend it on anything
oh, mighty green mountains!
oh, pallet of very useful shoehorns!

oh, cool winter breeze that somehow smells like a million baby sea turtles!

but also it's interesting to note that lovers' lane is just an imaginary street
and you will probably never find it in any of your toothbrushes from 1987

"really?
i just brushed my teeth
and i'm pretty sure i really thought it was there
hmmm that's odd"

and so you walk on past castle grayskull, past the movie theatre where they
serve up boiled peanuts and memories about war or prom night, past an
abandoned wig with a beer can growing out of it

"things just aren't a stuffed animal being coy on the telephone in a treehouse
with lyme disease anymore, are they," i remarked to my thermos the other day
while gently collapsing into a soothing baby pool full of demon blood

and the sun
is very pretty
when it goes away
and lets us be sad
on a mountaintop
with no cake or poultry around
anywhere at all

"my friends and family members
have no idea where i even am right now!
ha ha ha ha!"

WAFFLES

Well, hell, Bill wasn't doing anything so he decided to take a drive down to the Belgian waffle convention. Steve was going to be there which was a big bonus, maybe about the biggest bonus in the world since the Steve we're talking about here was, what, like maybe the best waffleman around. He'd made The Waffle That Is Impossible to Stop Eating, The Waffle that Turns You Instantly into Gonzo from the Muppets, The Waffle that Just Looks Like it's Made out of Cheese but it's Not. He also made normal conventional waffles that were normal and conventional but also so much better than anyone else's waffles that after having his, you kind of sort of really started to hate everybody else's waffles. That was where Bill was at in life at this point. He could really only eat Steve waffles or else puke in rage from eating someone else's waffles. Also, he sometimes had pumpkin pie as a treat. So, yeah, he drove downtown to the annual waffle convention hoping to find Steve right away, but he couldn't. "Steve! Steve!" said Bill, going around looking for Steve. He saw Brenda, Gill, and Todd "The Todd Monster" Michaelson, but no Bill. "Here have a Mint Chocolate Trunk Waffle," said Todd. "Did you say 'trunk'," said Bill. "Yes, I said 'trunk,'"said Todd. Bill ate the waffle. After the initial mint flavor, it gradually started to taste more like birch. "Oh, I get it," said Bill. But where was Steve? Bill threw up. He had almost forgotten to, but then he didn't. He was hoping he wouldn't have to resort to eating Todd waffles for the rest of his life. "My other surprise is the Funky Chicken Slime Waffle," said Todd. "Where's Steve?" said Bill. Todd pressed the Funky Chicken Slime waffle into Bill's mouth. Bill got all woozy. Something about it tasted kind of scary. Not just bad, but scary. Bill thought of possible reasons. Bill watched Todd scream around shoving huge weird waffles into other people's faces. Bill watched the specks of dried blood move around on Todd's face when he smiled. This was definitely a particularly competitive year at the waffle convention. The winner of the "best waffle" contest was supposed to get $50 and a new griddle.

A GOOD OLD-FASHIONED BUTT POEM

i put the movie on my butt

but where was my butt

my butt is from the future

it breathes new life into trumpets

a bright new spring day is my butt

if you were at the party, you probably saw my butt

no good life is complete without at least some kind of butt

my butt your butt bill's butt sally's butt the sun's butt the movie's butt

life is so wild + exciting + great that sometimes we forget that we all have butts

i know my butt like i know that butt, the one my lover has right where her butt is

no two butts are the same, every butt is unique and beautiful in some strange way

cloud butt robot butt serious butt angry butt loving butt kind butt butter butt smog butt roses butt

one time i fell asleep and my butt did too

good night butts

no, it is not time to party right now, butts; it is time to sleep

may your weariness eventually subside, like a butt that hath turned,
eventually, to dust

MAN IN THE MIRROR

It's like hearing the song "Man in the Mirror" by Michael Jackson while you are shopping for dental floss at a convenience store in Portland, Maine at 3a.m. What a positive and inspiring song! Back in the 1980's when it came out, it was actually briefly kind of fashionable to be a nice person and have lots of nice happy feelings. But now is the era of lonely unflavored soups and constant fear. The era of "if you're not a shiny million dollar evil robot who pays someone a full time wage to try and hide all of your natural flaws and mistakes, then you don't matter." What a perfect time to totally go against things and wear lots of really weird clothes. What a perfect time to smile at strangers and invite them over for a delicious and hearty spicy eggplant parmesan casserole of some kind. I have made so many mistakes in my life and have sometimes said some pretty mean things to maple trees. But also I hope to suddenly become a really awesome rainbow-colored unicorn that can jump up to the stars and get to all the secret control mechanisms of the universe. Once there, I will adjust things so that no one will ever be sad or angry or lonely or cruel ever again. I will adjust things until the beautiful Woolly Mammoth can come back to life and party with us all. And then maybe we'll all join hands and watch *Bill and Ted's Excellent Adventure* together. Or maybe *Weekend at Bernie's*. I haven't decided yet. It's so hard to pick out a good movie for everyone to enjoy. But if we all get into the spirit of things and there's popcorn made available and the promise of dancing in the backyard after the big sleepover movie in my Mom's TV room at my house in 1987 after a big day of skateboarding just for the fun of it in the park and complaining about math homework, then why can't we be happy and love each other for what we truly are without for a minute thinking that's corny. I love corny. I love love. And how can there ever be anything the least bit wrong with that?

ESSAY ON WALT WHITMAN

Walt Whitman played "The Star Spangled Banner" on an Olympic white Fender Stratocaster electric guitar in Woodstock, New York on Monday morning, August 18th, 1969 and changed the world forever.

Walt Whitman was also known as "Charlie Hustle" and hit a record breaking 3,215 singles during his 23 year career as a Major League switch-hitter before becoming "permanently banned from baseball" due to accusations that he had been gambling on his own team, The Cincinnati Reds.

Walt Whitman invented the wheel in 3500 B.C. in Mesopotamia, but at first he mainly only used it to make dumb pottery. It was at least a good 300 years later in Ancient Greece that he finally began using his wheel to totally kick major ass at chariot racing.

Walt Whitman is HD 140283, a 14 billion year old star nicknamed Methuselah, about 190 light years away from the planet you folks call "Earth."

Walt Whitman was definitely that crazy "spray on hair from a can" dude from those commercials that were always on TV when I was a kid in the early 1990's.

Walt Whitman was World War I, World War II, the sack of Babylon by the Hittites, the second Persian invasion of Greece, The Portuguese–Mamluk naval war, The War of the Quadruple Alliance, The Franco-Trarzan War of 1825, and pretty much every other stupid war that has ever existed for any stupid reason.

Walt Whitman is the loud bird who wakes me up at dawn each day and also the mellow happy feeling of "who cares?" that helps me to fall instantly back to sleep.

Walt Whitman loves it whenever a cartoon character wears a shrub as a disguise and then tiptoes around stealthily while a silly xylophone plays that funny sound that is supposed to apparently represent "sneaky footsteps."

Walt Whitman accidentally broke his leg while skateboarding on a gnarly half pipe in Santa Cruz, California in the summer of 1988.

Walt Whitman is the best damn slice of pumpkin pie Yankton, South Dakota has to offer.

Walt Whitman is a huge unexplored sea cave.

Walt Whitman likes long walks on the beach, professional wrestling, astrology, circuses, The National Geographic Society, any movie with Barbara Streisand in it, the occult, Christianity, Buddhism, Islam, peace, love, understanding, joy, sadness, evil, sex, mustard, lava, The Beatles, The Rolling Stones, and basically anything else that has ever existed or ever will.

I'M THE WORST GUITAR PLAYER EVER

i'm the worst guitar player ever.

sometimes my guitar solos are just

getting on a bus and going to

kentwood, michigan to

buy a hot dog.

one of my lives

before this life

was probably

selling yams

to people who already

have enough yams.

it's not enough in this world

to just have a pretty sneeze.

or, maybe sometimes it is.

there was this girl i once knew

who had the prettiest sneeze ever.

and also her shoes were carefully chosen.

her shoes weren't just any shoes.

i am telling you a story.

and she passed me a note

and i passed her a note

and it was almost better

than actually talking.

when i did talk, i said,

"i want to fall out of your car on purpose

and land on your driveway awkwardly

so that you can always help me live my life

which i do not know how to live."

in my imagination today she said,

"okay. let's do that plan. that is a pretty good plan."

and then she sneezed

and her sneeze reminded me of beautiful palm trees

quietly rustling in an ocean scented breeze.

but now life is different than that

because nothing really ever happened

between me and that sneeze girl.

she doesn't even know that i like her.

but tonight i will play for her

my absolute worst guitar solo ever.

for my worst guitar solo ever

i will just sit silently in this room

all alone

for hundreds and hundreds of years.

once in a while i might eat a cupcake.

but other than that,

i will probably just stick

with the doing of nothing.

BIOGRAPHY OF A LOST CAUSE

He never liked The Muppets.

He never ate a delicious flame-broiled cheeseburger.

He never combed the hair of a pretty young girl

And said, "There you go,

My little darling."

Mostly he just oiled his own muscles

Silently on a rock.

Or he performed an enormous number

Of impressive upside-down sit-ups

With his feet strapped up

To the ceiling

Of his old leaky houseboat

Parked on an icy

Oligotrophic lake

In Finland.

And he was always

Planning some kind of long sad trip to nowhere

That was also a contest

Where if he won

Somebody important was going to write his name

On a ledger

Buried in the sea

Inside a pirate's

Secret treasure chest

Guarded by a bunch of

Weird ferocious gigantic metal robot squids.

But if he lost,

He was just going to try and try again

No matter how boring or pointless

His life started to seem

To himself

Or to others.

His life was always just a giant eerie hill

That he was slowly learning how to climb.

DON'T ASK YOUR MOM TO PROM

the number of steves
who work at the library

who can count them all

there's not enough time

how many steves
are hiding out
in the book return box
right now
as i write this

some steves of course
get lost in the little
coin return slots
on the copy machines

people mostly use
the copy machines
to stand there
and cry about life

i am already tired of writing about steves!

except for steve buscemi

i want to buy him a big box
with a baby turtle inside

you know what i mean

and one man's plan
to wear sweatpants
for the rest of his life
was totally ruined

probably by a steve

that man's name is victor
and he is the only one who isn't a steve

his regular trousers
aren't that interesting

like drinking plain water
instead of having
a snappy and delicious
la croix
coconut flavored
sparkling water

jeff from omaha doesn't
work at my library

but still he is going to drive us to des moines
even though i only got 700 million points
on the theatre of magic
pinball machine
and probably smell like a
vast sausage and garlic
armpit universe

so what then
is life
really all about

certainly not steves!

but last night
when i was hardly sleeping at all
a new idea
suddenly climbed into bed with me
and made me feel
so young

and that idea
was to watch
golden girls reruns
on tv
and laugh at the way
our real lives
are always so much worse
than
the easy joy
of just watching tv

i don't even
know how to do my taxes
or have a conversation
that isn't awkward
and embarrassing
for us all

and sleep
how does anyone sleep????

thus, i came here to des moines

where the trees whisper
valuable secrets at you

whenever you are all alone
in front of the old
bowling supplies store

five dollars for the first minute
one dollar for each additional minute

IT'S AN EVIL MILLIONAIRE'S CHEST HAIR
YOU'RE TRYING TO DESCRIBE
WITH YOUR SILENT FACIAL EXPRESSIONS
AND I DON'T KNOW HOW YOU'RE GOING TO DO IT

those aren't the only nutritious cereal bars
that want you to wear slimy exam gloves
while you caress them and call them
stimpson j. cat

now dance in a tragic garden
you remember having a special moment in
during your youth

there are autumn leaves
all over your brother fred's
yahtzee dice game
and you've already used up
your one and only "chance" roll
so this time you'll have to go
with a really low score on your sixes
which means you'll also miss out on
the upper half bonus
which means you'll also bring shame and misery
to all of your descendents
if you're even lucky enough
to even have working sex parts at all
after this terrifically embarrassing
and low scoring game
where you'll definitely lose

listen, it's the time of your life all of the sudden
for no apparent reason

go to the rooftop garden party
dressed as the loneliest bowling trophy
ever to win a target gift card at a parish picnic

and, no,
the fun doesn't have to stop there
just because
we all live in des moines

there could also maybe be a small-ish
friendly get together
at a stupid shopping mall food court
where nobody smiles
and we all get to wish we were dead

DAD

at the same time, there is the desire to share your prayers with another human creature.

"we will make it to the top of hogsback mountain because you have nourished us with your many free peanut butter and jelly sandwiches, dad."

sometimes we would both wake up really early.

"your toothbrush is not the toothbrush that i would choose, but there it is sitting by the sink, ready to help you start your day."

i was going to go out west. you were going to "hold down the fort" beside lake michigan.

a cassette tape of herb alpert and the tijuana brass can hold a family together or just wait patiently inside a silver van.

your slippers on linoleum were like the puma i never saw lurking beside me in the desert.

sometimes you put your faith in neck warmers, kielbasa, and the baltimore orioles all at once!

i fixed my flat tire all by myself today and it hurt my head to let that happen.

you were always exercising in the basement with no lights on.

NORMAL STUPID MOON

normal stupid moon

just rising up

above a normal stupid tree

karate chop to the heart

deluxe turbo vacuum cleaner to the soul

great new fun christmas movie to the eyes

wow,

thanks a lot

normal stupid moon

you really made my day / night / whatever

ACTUALLY I ENJOY WEARING SWEATPANTS
MORE THAN I ENJOY FALLING IN LOVE

love is very interesting
but nobody knows
exactly what it is

so how can we even talk about it?

i fell asleep in the rain
and she kissed my face like i wasn't as ugly as i really am

i mowed the lawn for my
dead uncle's brother's roommate's cousin
even though i don't enjoy mowing lawns

these are just a few examples

perhaps you can think of some more examples on your own

then i won't have to work so hard
at trying to write a poem about love

but
there is a vague feeling
i get
that has nothing to do with myself sometimes

it wants only to help!
never to hurt!

it is a team player but wears no jersey

that's about all i know

love is so mysterious

it is a rare cloud that only follows one obscure spaceship above the yucky desert

but also it's everywhere at all times whenever anyone rolls up their sleeves

and puts in the effort

i love you love because you are never seen scolding happy hippies

or interrupting various beautiful music festivals

cause you're too doggone nice!

none of my selfish dreams involve you, love

please support all of my selfish dreams, love

"no, you're being stupid. even you hate your

own selfish dreams because they

only make you more miserable and pathetic

than you already are,"

says love

"oh yeah. that's right. i almost forgot.

let's go bake some cookies

for a bunch of woebegone

 mathletes" = love

and that's really good

at long last

a feeling

like melting
into a lime-green santa mug

oh love

you are everyone's favorite cup of tea

delicious, refreshing, new

who wouldn't care about you

if you were the last thing on earth besides pinecones

i do

MY PET BABY STARFISH IS GNARLIER THAN THE SONG CALLED "WIPEOUT" (KIND OF)

i guess i pretty much just like to watch a lot of weird old movies about weird old glove compartments and super scary super secret ghost swamps

but where are all the super scary super secret ghost swamps in this poem?????

i bet they ran away from me, ran away to find a better poem, a poem with huge insulting biceps and large congratulations from the mayor of montpelier

but then

"why, hello!" says one of them right now, ready to join up, ready to be a team player, ready to become a more cozy loveable reliable super secret super scary ghost swamp

"but where are you?" i ask

"the thing about me is that you can't see where i am and also i'm a swamp! ha ha!" says the super secret super scary ghost swamp, truly grabbing life by the horns

"i can't remember if you are just super scary or just super secret or both. i mean i keep changing my mind about what i want to remember. and also: got any rare oakland athletics rookie cards?" i say back, hoping to fulfill an old demolished dream about baseball cards.

remember baseball cards????

does anyone actually collect them anymore?

well, i sure don't

but a part of me right now kind of wishes that i could change this poem
so that it's only a baseball card poem,
only a poem about baseball cards and perhaps a few other things very closely
related to
baseball cards.

perhaps.

"no other thoughts allowed!" i say to the giant purple crayon i am writing this
with.

and then i start again.

"hmmm, baseball cards would make a pretty good topic for a poem"

. . . saturday afternoon walking downtown she carefully inspires everyone to
drop their tiny toy unicorns into the river and say goodbye to them and weep
because they are not baseball cards and neither are the tall blue buildings or
the stars in the sky that remind her of Herb, her dentist who she has a crush
on because his shoes always remain so sparkly like teeth, teeth in a dream
about baseball cards--her love knows no bounds! her love is a grand slam
home run hit by gary gaetti in 1987. everyone is impressed. they stand up in
the stands and don't think about church on sunday, they don't even think
about the game that they are watching, because oh no! their heads have
turned into baseball cards and their hot dogs have too. also there's a giant
stick of stale gum getting moldy in the sunlight like it wants to forget its days
of lying flat against a cardboard picture of nolan ryan getting ready to throw a
curveball at a yankee. his leg is weirdly bent up like he's a bird dancing in a

bird bath for fun! but what fun is it really to be a baseball card? your destiny
is: grandma's basement! "one of these days i'm going to get rid of everything
in the basement, but first: a round of bingo at saint alphonsus church!"

oh sleepy saturdays in the sunlight in the yard trading baseball cards
oh smell of beer and sound of AM radio static
oh cleats we wish we had

"if your pants aren't dirty at the end of the game
then you have probably wasted the game
and you are probably not
on a baseball card" says Coach Hillary to the burlap bag of bats we used to
have to carry on our tiny fourth grade shoulders

but why is he talking to the bats

and why is he even in this poem

he is not a baseball card

and i definitely don't even say hi to him anymore

he lives far away

in a beaver den on the swift river in belchertown, massachusetts

where every day he must swim underwater for a bit

to get out of the beaver den

that contains

exactly two and a half ricky henderson baseball cards

a widow gifted them to the beavers

during a special fancy ceremony

involving cherry limeade,
a bit of her dead husband's lusty ashes,
and a bunch of other cool stuff
i don't have time to list here right now

i mean remember when we all used to dream super big

"man i was so proud of hitting that homer

the baseball just flew and flew until it hit some guy in the head way over in
the convenience store parking lot

what a lucky day!

now i just work in a lumberyard and sweat and eat bland oatmeal that i don't
even like that much

oh well

at least i got my housecat named Fond Duke Hissington the Third. . . . "

sad cat mean cat bad cat other kinds of cats

just shrug it off

the way a guy on a baseball card would

swinging fifty bats

as a way to warm up

for swinging only one bat

HOW TO BE MY FAVORITE PERSON EVER

yodel barry manilow songs at a tall slimy ham hock

invent five hundred new ways of thoroughly enjoying clearance bin sweatpants

bring back the sacred joy of wearing hockey masks to the opera house

say something rude to an enormous barrel of salad tongs

roll around in a giant field full of frosting

describe your earwax to a stranger

win every award and honor that can ever be given in the discipline of calligraphy

make out with a dinette set and then marry a casserole dish

grow out your nose hair until it starts to look like a really cool moustache

tell me i am your real live dinosaur friend whenever i am pretending to be your real live dinosaur friend

IT IS DEFINITELY GOOD FUN
TO PUT ON A WEIRD SMOCK AND PRETEND
TO BE A WISE OLD SEA CAPTAIN
BUT I BET THAT ACTUAL SEA CAPTAINS
HAVE TO ENDURE SOME PRETTY TERRIBLE STUFF

i love when drunk steve buscemi in a tuxedo says "i'm the best guitar player in the world!!!!!!!!!!!" in the movie *the wedding singer*

i remember when i first saw *the wedding singer*

i was in eighth grade and i still believed in love

jacob caya had donuts for lunch and we all thought it was normal

matt iacopelli probably had a candy bar

i had an egg salad sandwich, i think

then we saw the movie and i thought, "i'm going to meet billy idol on an airplane too someday!!!!!!!!!!!!

and i'm going to teach an old lady to sing 'till there was you even though she pays me only in meatballs"

actually none of those things have ever happened to me

and i'm not still in eighth grade either

i'm in, like, old guy grade

where every day is the same and it seems exciting just to eat your eggs while watching a squirrel outside

i guess that something is probably breaking inside of me

i walk to work and think i see a carton of orange juice playing a banjo in a tree

or a secret spaceship where f. scott fitzgerald is the driver and he's also making out with a snowman

years and years go by

i think of beautiful downtowns where i dreamed of doing something really interesting

but then i just got a job and ate dinner and went to sleep like everybody else

not toooooo interesting

the trains on the railroad at night: choooo choooo!

they are trying to tell me something

"come out into the moonlight

come dance naked on a trampoline

swim with the sharks

pour whiskey on your head

wrestle a cheesecake for money

become a fucking wizard and breathe magic spells onto troubled nations to promote world peace and love

but where is love when you're basically a robot and don't even choose which can of soup you pour into your microwave at night

microwave of doom

microwave of gloom

why cook so fast

there's a pretty girl inside your heart glowing like champagne. . . . "

so, yeah, that's what the trains are saying

and it makes me feel so fucking lonely

like i will never get a letter back from my favorite pen pal

like i'm a lost forgotten table saw in the back of somebody's messy garage and i will never ever get a chance to sing or dance or make love or cough into a really cool handkerchief, one of those ones with little cowboy patterns on it or maybe tiny dots, i don't know

THERE ARE APPROXIMATELY ZERO ASTONISHING FACTS ABOUT RIBOFLAVIN OR OTHER B VITAMINS IN THIS POEM

Years go by. Sometimes you mow a lawn. Sometimes you buy pants with discount coupons. You think smiles are nice, especially on ducks, but is that duck actually smiling or does it only seem like it is smiling? "I'll have ten huge burritos to go." Nobody at the restaurant knows that you live alone and are going to use the burritos to survive for a week without leaving the house. Some beautiful mysteries echo deep within your bones. But nobody can see them, so it feels like a waste. But what if a stranger with x-ray eyes has actually seen them? There is no way to know. You could ride a boat to some faraway place, arrive there feeling very happy, and still not know anything about anyone at all. Spices can be used in so many different ways. Animals are not the same as plants. Musical instruments are only boring if you bury them in a sandbox full of sand. But why would you ever do that? I mean: your years could go by so much differently. Why have you been wasting all of your years? You could have been a pink and purple flower with a bunch of zig zagging lightning bolts tattooed on your sepal. You could have been a really fun roller coaster that goes nowhere but at least lets people have lots of fun while they are going to nowhere. So why not dust those corn chip crumbs off your hilarious he-man pjs and rise! Rise like a gorgeous sockeye salmon leaping courageously into some random grizzly bear's mouth, totally ready for anything: hurrah!

ACKNOWLEDGEMENTS

Thank you thank you thank you to anyone who helped in any way to make this ridiculous book possible!!!!! (!!!!!) Especially: Kyle McCord, Nick Courtright, and Margo at Gold Wake Press, the artist LK James, Ma and Pa Flak, all my friends and family members, everyone at the Grand Rapids Public Library, everyone at Skipfiction, everyone at Maudlin House, everyone from Whale Prom, everyone from The Drunken Retort at Stella's Lounge, everyone from Mayan Buzz All Access Open Mic, James Haug, James Tate, Stanley Crawford, Dara Wier, Jennifer L. Knox, Tim Staley, Johnny Huerta, Jimmy Stewart, Buster Keaton, John Hughes, Brian Wilson, John Cusack, Steve Buscemi, Calvin Johnson from K Records, the rock group McWeakerton, Ronald Johnson, Matt Hudson, Dan Welling, Jeff Alessandrelli, Michael Sikkema, Jen Tynes, Kyra Van Horn, Ozzy the dog, Victor Puhy, Christina Aderholdt, Jeanne Clemo, and everyone else in the whole entire universe.

Versions of some of the poems in this book may have first appeared:

in *Bat City Review, Hart House Review, jubilat, Skipfiction, watermelon isotope*, and various other magazines, websites, journals, etc.

in the chapbook *What Hank Said on the Bus* (Publishing Genius, 2013) (Winner of the Chris Toll Prize)

in my MFA in poetry thesis at UMass Amherst, *Escape from the Haunted City of Fright and Doom!* (Scholarworks, 2011)

as live performances at Stella's Lounge, the Mayan Buzz Cafe, and at various Skipfiction house shows

my prose poem about Walt Whitman first appeared on the blog for Hunter Lee Hughes' independent film *Guys Reading Poems*

The poem now called "DON'T ASK YOUR MOM TO PROM" first appeared as "THE NUMBER OF STEVES WHO WORK AT THE LIBRARY" in *Bat City Review*.

"MY VERSION OF AWESOME KARATE IS JUST EATING POPCORN ALONE IN A SEWER WITH MY DAD'S OLD CATCHER'S MITT FOR A BOWL" was first performed by a robot on a Skipfiction podcast. Thank you to Schyler Perkins and John Akers for making that robot do that.

"A GOOD OLD-FASHIONED BUTT POEM" is basically just my own pathetic rewrite of the great and famous "Hot Ass Poem" by Jennifer L. Knox. Her poem existed before mine did.

MY PET BABY STARFISH IS GNARLIER THAN THE SONG CALLED "WIPEOUT" (KIND OF) was first performed in Michael Sikkema and Jen Tynes' backyard on a cool summer evening.

ABOUT GOLD WAKE PRESS

Gold Wake Press, an independent publisher, is curated by Nick Courtright and Kyle McCord. All Gold Wake titles are available at amazon.com, barnesandnoble.com, and via order from your local bookstore. Learn more at goldwake.com. Here are some of our recent titles:

Brandon Amico's *Disappearing, Inc.*
Dana Diehl and Melissa Goodrich's *The Classroom*
Sarah Strickley's *Fall Together*
Andy Briseño's *Down and Out*
Talia Bloch's *Inheritance*
Eileen G'Sell's *Life After Rugby*
Erin Stalcup's *Every Living Species*
Glenn Shaheen's *Carnivalia*
Frances Cannon's *The High and Lows of Shapeshift Ma and Big-Little Frank*
Justin Bigos' *Mad River*
Kelly Magee's *The Neighborhood*
Kyle Flak's *I Am Sorry for Everything in the Whole Entire Universe*
David Wojciechowski's *Dreams I Never Told You & Letters I Never Sent*
Keith Montesano's *Housefire Elegies*
Mary Quade's *Local Extinctions*
Adam Crittenden's *Blood Eagle*
Lesley Jenike's *Holy Island*
Mary Buchinger Bodwell's *Aerialist*
Becca J. R. Lachman's *Other Acreage*
Joshua Butts' *New to the Lost Coast*
Tasha Cotter's *Some Churches*
Hannah Stephenson's *In the Kettle, the Shriek*
Nick Courtright's *Let There Be Light*
Kyle McCord's *You Are Indeed an Elk, but This Is Not the Forest You Were Born to Graze*

ABOUT THE AUTHOR

KYLE FLAK enjoys handwriting weird stuff in cheap notebooks just for the fun of it. His previous book from Gold Wake Press was called *I am Sorry for Everything in the Whole Entire Universe*. His writing has recently appeared in various literary magazines like *Bat City Review, jubilat, Mudfish, Poetry East, Spinning Jenny*, and *Whiskey Island*. He also performs his work in public at various indie rock house shows, open mic nights, and literary events. He grew up in Grand Rapids, Michigan and went to school at Northern Michigan University and the University of Massachusetts at Amherst.

CPSIA information can be obtained
at www.ICGtesting.com
Printed in the USA
FSHW010740060220
66634FS